I0167110

FIG Leaves

By A. Russell

"Covering up "DA" sexy in a sexually saturated society"

A Bold Call to Modesty and Purity

A. Russell, Author
Illustrations: Aleria M. Hurks & Robert Russell
Typesetting, Layout, & Design: Ida M. Jackson
Printing: DiggyPod.com ● U.S.A. 2014

ISBN: 978-0-692-24794-5

> *But among you there must not be even a hint of sexual immorality, or of any kind of impurity, or of greed, because these are improper for God's holy people.* —Ephesians 5:3 New International Version (NIV)

DEFINITIONS:

Modest: Having or showing regard for decencies of behavior, speech, dress; (decent).

Immodest: Lacking modesty—Offending against sexual mores in conduct or appearance (indecent); Not properly restrained in expression or self-assertion; Imprudent or shameless.

Decent: Conforming with generally accepted standards of respectable or moral behavior. Of an acceptable standard; satisfactory.

Indecent: Not conforming with generally accepted standards of behavior or propriety; obscene.

Not appropriate or fitting, improper, unseemly, unbecoming, unladylike, racy, unsuitable, tasteless, inappropriate, offensive.

Scantily Clad: *Scantily:* Limited, barely enough, meagre, insufficient; inadequate. *Clad:* clothing.

Sin: Transgression of the Law (breaking God's laws).

Lawlessness: A person who breaks, violates, disobeys or transgresses the law.

Willful Disobedience: Deliberate in action.

Willful Ignorance: Lack of knowledge, but goes ahead with plans in spite of consequences.

Obedience: relates to hearing or hearkening to a higher authority. It also conveys the concept of submission and trust.

Table of Contents

PREFACE

It was never my intention to write a book—ever! However, the Lord convicted my spirit to reach out in written form to address the issue of modesty and how it has lost its way in today's society. It has literally become "taboo" to broach upon the subject for fear of "political incorrectness."

Writing a book about how a woman should or should not dress may not be well received. After all, who am I to talk about what a woman should or should not wear? It's a free country, right? Nevertheless, I stand willing and ready to receive criticism about my boldness.

Despite our desire to avoid talking about what is or is not acceptable apparel, these are conversations that need to be had—not just for the good of our personal Christian walks, but also for the good of our men and children.

Oftentimes, we fail to recognize that many of our choices can affect others emotionally, physically, mentally, and socially. What we wear says a lot to others about who we are as a person; and, we must always remember that the first impression is the greatest. It is noteworthy to mention that people are going to judge us by the old saying *"If it looks like a duck, walks like a duck, and quacks like a duck, then it must be a duck."*

For example, as a woman, I must be cognizant of what I wear when I visit my child's school because it directly affects how my child is perceived by his peers and teachers. If I visit his school wearing a scantily clad, tightly fitted dress or my pajamas or a robe, then my child will feel an embarrassment and shame that only **my change** in lifestyle choices can eliminate.

If I don't change my perception of what is appropriate to wear in public, then my child will suffer the consequences of my bad choices and consequently, may choose to follow in my footsteps and become an embarrassment to me later in life.

In our attempts to be accepting, it seems as if we might have become too liberal, allowing ourselves to wear whatever we want to wear and however we want to wear it. When we get to this point in our lives, we need to realize that our clothing has become a product of our **environment** instead of a reflection of our convictions and beliefs.

DEDICATION

This book is dedicated to my husband, sons, and brothers in Christ. May you always strive to be men and young men of faith, integrity, and character; vowing to be **Job 31** men (making a covenant with your eyes) and living lives of purity in obedience to Christ and his commandments, in the midst of a world that loves darkness and unholy living. Stay strong and be encouraged.

To my daughters and sisters in Christ, always strive to be clothed in a manner worthy of representing Him, witnessing to a lost and dying world by your very appearance. Thereby honoring God as did the **virtuous** woman.

~ ~

John 14:21 (Men and Women) Whomever has my commands and keeps them is the one who loves me.

1 Corinthians 6:19-20 (Ladies) Do you not know that your bodies are temples of the Holy Spirit who is in you, whom you have received from God? You are not your own; you were bought at a price.

Psalm 119:11 (Men) How can a young man keep his way pure? By guarding it according to your word. With my whole heart I seek you; let me not wonder from your commandments! I have **stored up your words in my heart**, that I might not sin against you.

Virtuous: having or showing high moral standards; pure, upright, chaste.

Proverb 31:10-31 1The words of king Lemuel, the prophecy that his mother taught him. ² What, my son? and what, the son of my womb? and what, the son of my vows? ³ Give not thy strength unto women, nor thy ways to that which destroyeth kings. ⁴ It is not for kings, O Lemuel, it is not for kings to drink wine; nor for princes strong drink: ⁵ Lest they drink, and forget the law, and pervert the judgment of any of the afflicted. ⁶ Give strong drink unto him that is ready to perish, and wine unto those that be of heavy hearts. ⁷ Let him drink, and forget his poverty, and remember his misery no more. ⁸ Open thy mouth for the dumb in the cause of all such as are appointed to destruction. ⁹ Open thy mouth, judge righteously, and plead the cause of the poor and needy. ¹⁰ Who can find a virtuous woman? for her price is far above rubies. ¹¹ The heart of her husband doth safely trust in her, so that he shall have no need of spoil. ¹² She will do him good and not evil all the days of her life. ¹³ She seeketh wool, and flax, and worketh willingly with her hands. ¹⁴ She is like the merchants' ships; she bringeth her food from afar. ¹⁵ She riseth also while it is yet night, and giveth meat to her household, and a portion to her maidens. ¹⁶ She considereth a field, and buyeth it: with the fruit of her hands she planteth a vineyard. ¹⁷ She girdeth her loins with strength, and strengtheneth her arms. ¹⁸ She perceiveth that her merchandise is good: her candle goeth not out by night. ¹⁹ She layeth her hands to the spindle, and her hands hold the distaff. ²⁰ She stretcheth out her hand to the poor; yea, she reacheth forth her hands to the needy. ²¹ She is not afraid of the snow for her household: for all her household are clothed with scarlet. ^{22} She maketh herself coverings of tapestry; her clothing is silk and purple. ^{23} Her husband is known in the gates, when he sitteth among the elders of the land. ^{24} She maketh fine linen, and selleth it; and delivereth girdles unto the merchant. ^{25} Strength and honour are her clothing; and she shall rejoice in time to come. ^{26} She openeth her mouth with wisdom; and in her tongue is the law of kindness. ^{27} She looketh well to the ways of her household, and eateth not the bread of idleness. ^{28} Her children arise up, and call her blessed; her husband also, and he praiseth her. ^{29} Many daughters have done virtuously, but thou excellest them all. ^{30} Favour is deceitful, and beauty is vain: but a woman that feareth the LORD, she shall be praised. ^{31} Give her of the fruit of her hands; and let her own works praise her in the gates.

In The Beginning—
"Before The Fall"

Genesis 2:15-25 New International Version (NIV)

[15] The LORD God took the man and put him in the Garden of Eden to work it and take care of it. [16] And the LORD God commanded the man, "You are free to eat from any tree in the garden; [17] but you must not eat from the tree of the knowledge of good and evil, for when you eat from it you will certainly die."

[18] The LORD God said, "It is not good for the man to be alone. I will make a helper suitable for him."

[19] Now the LORD God had formed out of the ground all the wild animals and all the birds in the sky. He brought them to the man to see what he would name them; and whatever the man called each living creature, that was its name. [20] So the man gave names to all the livestock, the birds in the sky and all the wild animals.

But for Adam[f] no suitable helper was found. [21] So the LORD God caused the man to fall into a deep sleep; and while he was sleeping, he took one of the man's ribs[g] and then closed up the place with flesh. [22] Then the LORD God made a woman from the rib[h] he had taken out of the man, and he brought her to the man.

[23] The man said, "This is now bone of my bones
     and flesh of my flesh;
she shall be called 'woman,'
     for she was taken out of man."

[24] That is why a man leaves his father and mother and is united to his wife, and they become one flesh.

[25] Adam and his wife were both naked, and they felt no shame.

God planted a garden in Eden and He put Adam and Eve there to live. He gave them everything that they could possibly want or need. Every tree was aesthetically pleasing to the eye and good to eat, except the two trees that He planted in the middle of the garden—the tree of good and evil and the tree of life!

He gave Adam specific instructions about these two trees before He made Eve from one of Adam's ribs. He warned him about the consequence of death should he disobey the Lord by eating from the trees. So Adam knew from the very beginning that these two trees were never to be touched by anyone!

God did not interfere with their free will. He gave them the same thing that He gives us all — choice. Imagine the fragrant smells of the fruit and vegetables in the garden of Eden. Each with its own distinct flavor. They could choose to eat what their hearts desired. They had no need to eat from the tree of good and evil.

Satan comes in many forms and his goal is to get revenge on God for banishing him from heaven. His given name in heaven was Lucifer, and he was an important angel, but he got the "big head," and decided that he would dethrone God.

It's always been said that misery loves company! So, it's no big surprise that he wants to recruit all of the children of man (Adam). He's cunning and deceitful and he used his wily ways to convince Adam's wife Eve to partake of the tree of good and evil. His lies caused Eve's eyes to be opened and she knew that she had done wrong because now she is able to discern what is good and what is evil! Remember, misery loves company! She in turn convinced her husband to eat the fruit of the tree and his eyes became open to his surrounding and he knew the difference between good and evil.

Those two trees represented God's authority and His desire to shield His creations from death and evil. The choices we make as mothers, daughter, and sisters are ours to make whether good or bad. But, we must remember that with the choice to be disobedient comes bad consequences and a price to be paid for our sins.

He always wishes for his children to be obedient, and has outlined a life for us through his Word (The Bible). He wants us to live clean lives and has given us a map, from start to finish, as to how to carry out Godly living. Let us take heed to His warnings about our chosen lifestyles as we come before His presence daily.

The Fall—
Temptation/Deception

Genesis 3:1-6 (NIV)

3 Now the serpent was more crafty than any of the wild animals the LORD God had made. He said to the woman, "Did God really say, 'You must not eat from any tree in the garden'?"

² The woman said to the serpent, "We may eat fruit from the trees in the garden, ³ but God did say, 'You must not eat fruit from the tree that is in the middle of the garden, and you must not touch it, or you will die.'"

⁴ "You will not certainly die," the serpent said to the woman. ⁵ "For God knows that when you eat from it your eyes will be opened, and you will be like God, knowing good and evil."

⁶ When the woman saw that the fruit of the tree was good for food and pleasing to the eye, and also desirable for gaining wisdom, she took some and ate it. She also gave some to her husband, who was with her, and he ate it.

I Corinthians 10:13 (paraphrased) says that there is no temptation on earth that's new to man, so in other words, it's all old school, and we can overcome all temptations that life throws our way, with God's help. There are no new temptations that God does not know about, for He knows them all and is always there waiting to help us pass the test—if we desire to pass it.

Should there be no desire to pass it, then man will just waddle in the pleasures of sin (James 1:15). Ultimately, waddling in the pleasures of sin gives birth to death. Satan always has a way to make sin look glamorous; however, no matter how pleasing a thing may appear, taste, or feel, our Heavenly Father calls upon us to not be a part of it.

We, as Christians, have the responsibility to resist temptations through prayer and guidance from the Holy Spirit. We should never hesitate to remove ourselves from situations or environments that may present themselves as stumbling blocks in our own struggles with a specific temptation. For example, even though we try to help a brother or sister with a lustful sin, if we are struggling with the same temptation, we do them a disservice, because we are not strong enough to share their burden. Be wise and seek another to help that brother or sister.

No matter how much a sinner or "sinning professing Christians" are enjoying the pleasures of sin for a season, God knows the heart, and every knee must bow and one day give account for every idle word and sinful deeds.

And for those who say they don't go to church or live like "Christians" because Christians are hypocrites; I say, live your life in accordance to His Word by attending a good Bible based church and leave the mess to the sinners/

hypocrites. For surely, there are many hypocrites that warm church seats and pews on Sunday mornings; however, be assured that there will be no hypocrites in heaven. So make sure you are not there in hell to greet them at the door! God desires all his children to repent and not just be hearers of his word but rather hearers and doers.

The bottom line is that all un-repented sin leads to death, which is a promise from God to us all. He also goes on to say in Matthew 7:21-23 (summarized) that "not everyone who says to me, Lord, Lord, will enter into the kingdom of heaven. Only those who do the will of my father." The Word says that He will say "Depart from me, I NEVER KNEW YOU."

These are words that many don't think they will hear on that day; however, the Bible makes it clear that they will. I know that I don't want to see a serial killer who has not repented of his sins, living alongside me in heaven. He truly belongs with his mentor, satan! Only God knows the heart and only He can judge who is truly repentant of his sins.

The Bible tells us plainly that no man knows the time or the day when Jesus is going to return, so it behooves us all to live our lives as if He's coming back in a flash! Revelations tells us the kinds of people who will be sent to their deaths and serial killers are not the only un-repentant sinners. Jezebel and all of the Jezebels of this world will be joining them!

So, don't follow the narcissistic example that Eve set before us when we deal with our husbands and God. We can change our appearance, but we must change our views about life first, and that change comes only by our commitment to serve the Lord with all of our hearts, souls, and minds.

16

Ask Rehab, the Samaritan woman at the well, and the woman with the alabaster box how changing their sinful lifestyles to a holy lifestyle changed their personal relationship with Christ!

Eyes Wide Open

Genesis 3:7 (NIV)

[7] Then the eyes of both of them were opened, and they realized they were naked; so they sewed fig leaves together and made coverings for themselves.

Genesis 3:7 (KJV)

[7] And the eyes of them both were opened, and they knew that they were naked; and they sewed **fig leaves** together, and made themselves **aprons.**

Genesis 3:21 (KJV)

[21] Unto Adam also and to his wife did the LORD God make **coats of skins**, and clothed them.

Before they ate of the tree of good and evil, Adam and Eve did not have lustful thoughts, no thoughts of killing and eating animals, and no thoughts of murdering each other. They did not live in fear and their lives were peaceful. Nothing in the garden could harm them.

But, because of their disobedience, their eyes were opened to all wickedness and sin. Life as it had been would be no more. You see, they no longer had the innocence of new born babies. They were now full grown adults who began to experience the desires and feelings associated with being a man and a woman. When they looked upon each other, they felt the shame that we feel today when we see another unclothed person. Babies can run around naked and think nothing about it because they have no knowledge of good and evil. When we grow into men and women, our nakedness is attached to carnal pleasure. That is why it is said that we are conceived in sin, because our innocence will ultimately give way to carnality.

When they looked upon each other after eating the fruit, they knew that it had somehow changed how they felt about each other. Their feelings were now new and different. To cover the embarrassment and shame they felt, they tried to "put some clothes on their bodies," to cover their nakedness.

In their attempt to "put on some cloths," the Bible (KJV) says (**Genesis 3:7**) *"And the eyes of them both were opened, and they knew that they were naked; and they sewed fig leaves together, and made themselves aprons."* It is common knowledge that aprons usually serve to cover the front part of the body from the waist down to the upper thighs. Apparently, they did not have time or did not know how to cover themselves fully when they heard the voice of

God walking in the garden, so they ran and hid.

When God found them, they feigned stupidity and played the "blame game," just as we do today when we are caught in sinful acts or situations. Adam blamed his wife and his wife blamed the serpent, but God held them all responsible for their horrific sin of disobedience!

This is why we, as women, have to take responsibility for our own lifestyles. We cannot blame the world and say "*A lot of other women dress this way.*"

I don't believe that it was the fact that they were naked before God that made Him angry, because they had been naked since He created them. I believe that the fact that they knew that they were naked angered Him <u>and</u> that they had lost their innocence because they had broken His first commandment of <u>obedience</u> **and** committed the first sin—<u>deceitfulness</u>.

They disobeyed God and consequently, they tried to deceive Him by hiding their acts of disobedience. God knew that from this single act of sin of deceitfulness, that more sin would ensue—including, but not limited to: murder, lying, adultery, fornication, whoredom, lust, homosexuality, and et cetera.

I believe that God covered them fully because their nakedness represented their willful disregard for God's gift of life to them. It is much like our children when they've gotten older and want to live their lives contrary to our Biblical teachings. We love them, but they have to leave our house until they can honor the rules of our home. Adam and Eve had to leave God's garden.

The Bible says that He clothed them in coats of skin. It

is this writer's thoughts that this was done to show them and to help them to understand that in their new lifestyles, they would have to fend for themselves by killing animals for food, shelter, and clothing—to help make sense of their new world and how He would be there to help and guide them through it. I truly believe that He wanted them to know that whether they were in the garden or in the world that they were still in His presence and that their discovery of their nakedness was the beginning of all lustful desires. He expected for them to dress appropriately and demonstrated it by supplying them with coats.

We as women, must fully dress ourselves when entering God's house. Not being fully clothed is indicative of bringing the world into the house of the Lord. He didn't want Adam and Eve naked in His garden because of all the temptations that it might present and He doesn't want nakedness in His House of Prayer for the same reasons. He is not pleased when we come into His House with low-cut tops, Daisy Duke styled shorts, pants showing our buttocks, and tightly fitted clothing. **This kind of nakedness is akin to covering oneself with fig leaves,** because it only serves to perpetuate other carnal lusts within the House of God.

Additionally, Christian women should know that not only should they dress appropriately in God's house of prayer, but in public as well, because it is not Godly or a good witness to the world.

Revelation 2:20 says *"Notwithstanding I have a few things against thee, because thou sufferest that woman Jezebel, which calleth herself a prophetess, to teach and to* *seduce my servants to commit fornication, and to eat things sacrificed unto idols. "*

This Bible verse is the very reason we are called to cover our bodies according to God's standards, and not our own or the world's.

Not Even A Hint—Fast forward to the year 2014

Ephesians 5:3-5— (NIV)

[3] But among you there must not be even a hint of sexual immorality, or of any kind of impurity, or of greed, because these are improper for God's holy people. [4] Nor should there be obscenity, foolish talk or coarse joking, which are out of place, but rather thanksgiving. [5] For of this you can be sure: No immoral, impure or greedy person—such a person is an idolater—has any inheritance in the kingdom of Christ and of God

Ephesians 5:3-5—(KJV)

[3] But fornication, and all uncleanness, or covetousness, let it not be once named among you, as becometh saints; [4] Neither filthiness, nor foolish talking, nor jesting, which are not convenient: but rather giving of thanks. [5] For this ye know, that no whoremonger, nor unclean person, nor covetous man, who is an idolater, hath any inheritance in the kingdom of Christ and of God.

Ida Malone Jackson, a local author and friend of mine, wrote this perspective in her book **By Thought, Word, and Deed**, *"The devil has made the <u>female angel graven image</u>, the angel of our God and we have accepted it as the Gospel truth. Television commercials glorify them and they are portrayed down the runways as women in scanty and sexual attire."*

Ephesians 5:3 tells us that the world revels in sexiness, <u>but among Christians there must not even be a **hint** of sexiness, immorality, or impurity of any kind.</u>

When we as women dress provocatively, we are hinting that we are willing, ready, and available for all that a man is able to provide. Some women dress to please the husbands, boyfriends, or fiancées **of other women** without regard for the institution of marriage or relationships.

Many unprincipled women will say "She doesn't own him," or "If she doesn't give him what he needs, I will." This hint may include cooking for the man, doing special little favors for him, siding with him about marital problems, dressing so that he lusts after her with his eyes, body language, or speech, and pretending to be helpless and need his personal attention. Corinthians 6:19-20 says *"Do you not know that your bodies are temples of the Holy Spirit, who is in you, whom you have received from God? You are not your own; you were bought with a price. Therefore honor God with your bodies."*

We as Christian Women and young ladies are instructed by God to cover up and be modest. Modest in character, conversation, and conduct. Even the smallest **hint** that may cause others to stumble in the House of God or in the world, by those who profess to follow the teachings of Jesus Christ, is a dangerous game to play with the Lord.

SUPPLY AND DEMANDS
You want it!
I have it!
You Can Get It!

But it comes with a price!
Leave Your Wife
Leave Your Family
Leave Your Church

Public Display of Affections!

Potty Mouth!

GOSSIPING
Don't start no mess,
won't be no mess!

God's Warnings—To Men and Women, Young Ladies and Young Men

DON'T WRECK YOUR LIFE!

GOD'S WARNINGS

These warnings can go either way, however males in general, typically have issues with lust; whereas, females (and younger males) usually have issues with inappropriate choices in clothing.

Mathew 5:27-28 (NIV)— [27] "You have heard that it was said, 'You shall not commit adultery.'[a] [28] But I tell you that anyone who looks at a woman lustfully has already committed adultery with her in his heart.

Luke 17:1— Jesus said to his disciples: "Things that cause people to stumble are bound to come, but woe to anyone through whom they come.

Proverbs 7:10 "Then came a woman to meet him dressed like a prostitute and with crafty intent" (Paraphrased—skimpy/revealing clothing out to set a trap of seduction)

1 Peter 3:3 "Your beauty should not come from outward adornments."

Holman Christian Standard Bible: "Also, the women are to dress themselves in modest clothing, with decency and good sense"   .

King James Bible: "In like manner also, the women adorn themselves in modest apparel, with shamefacedness and sobriety."

Proverbs 7:10 "And behold, there met him a woman with attire of an harlot."

Harlot —A prostitute or promiscuous woman.
Harlot attire—Clothing designed to seduce men.

The Bible clearly recognizes that there are particular styles of dressing for harlots or women of ill repute. **My prayer is that all women will read and understand that Christianity does not only lie in the mind, but in one's physical appearance.** Many Christians have been brainwashed by this fallacy or notion that Christianity only lies in the mind. How can a woman dress provocatively and say, "Oh, Christianity is one's mindset."

A prostitute is a person whose main product is the body. The way a prostitute dresses advertises the sensitive parts of the body to enhance the marketable value of herself wherever she goes, and is not limited to only hotels and the streets. The dressing choices of a harlot is revealing, suggestive, sexy, seductive, and provocative.

One Man's Voice on Women and Modesty

It is a given that people as a whole are going to break the laws of the land and the laws of God. Jesus tells us in Matthew 22:21 *that we are to render unto Caesar the things which are Caesar's; and unto God the things that are God's.* If we break the laws of the land, we will be punished by those who govern us. If we break God's commandments, God will surely punish us.

You might ask "Are not God's laws and the government laws the same?" No, not necessarily. For example, in **Leviticus, 18:22** it says "Thou shalt not lie with mankind, as with womankind: it is abomination and **Leviticus, 20:13** "If man also lie with **mankind**, as he lieth with a woman, both of them have committed an abomination: they shall surely be put to death; their blood shall be upon them. However, the laws of the land sanctions same sex marriages and have no laws which forbid having sexual intimacy between two consenting adults. In this case, Christians must remember that we cannot serve both man and God.

Just because the laws of the land do not forbid or punish men for solely lusting after women in their hearts or women for scantily clad garments (provocatively) in public, it does not mean that God will not judge them. It is generally noted that most men are visual creatures; and, yes, looking at women in lustful ways is a major fault of theirs. However, it must also be noted that many women dress in such a way that they invite the lustful stares of men.

We have a high calling to not live like the world. There should not be even a hint of unholy choices. The Word of God should govern all of our choices, decisions, and actions. There should not even be a hint of questionable intake as to what we let our eyes look upon. Even in stolen moments, a look or glance can have long-lasting affects upon our minds and our thinking—movies, magazines, television, internet, books and et cetera. Not even a hint of inquiry as to what goes on, not even a hint.

"There should not even be a hint of suggestiveness or inappropriateness in our dress. We should always consider the impact of our appearance on others—our brothers, our children, and a watching world. And of course, on how we represent our Lord.

I Timothy 4:12 *"Set an example for the believers in speech, in conduct, in love, in faith and in purity."*

As pointed out in the story about Jezebel, just as a Man will answer to God for his lustful ways, a woman will have to answer to God for her part in causing him to stumble.

Dressing For Success
As
A Promiscuous Woman

Temptations

Psalm 119:9-11 (ESV)

[9] How can a young man keep his way pure? By guarding it according to your word. [10] With my whole heart I seek you; let me not wander from your commandments! [11] I have stored up your word in my heart, that I might not sin against you.

1 Corinthians 10:13 (KJV)

13 There hath no temptation taken you but such as is common to man: but God is faithful, who will not suffer you to be tempted above that ye are able; but will with the temptation also make a way to escape, that ye may be able to bear it.

James 1:2-4

[2] Consider it pure joy, my brothers and sisters whenever you face trials of many kinds, [3] because you know that the testing of your faith produces perseverance. [4] Let perseverance finish its work so that you may be mature and complete, not lacking anything.

Ephesians 6:12 (KJV)

12 For we wrestle not against flesh and blood, but against principalities, against powers, against the rulers of the darkness of this world, against spiritual *wickedness in high places.*

2 Corinthians 10:3-6 (NIV)

[3] For though we live in the world, we do not wage war as the world does. [4] The weapons we fight with are not the weapons of the world. On the contrary, they have divine power to demolish strongholds. [5] We demolish arguments and every pretension that sets itself up against the

knowledge of God, and we take captive every thought to make it obedient to Christ. [6] And we will be ready to punish every act of disobedience, once your obedience is complete.

The Bible **doesn't say** that temptation is a sin, **but rather,** when we <u>give in</u> to temptation, **that's when** it becomes a sin. Jesus <u>was being tempted</u> to sin.

The gospel accounts in Matthew and Luke explicitly describe Jesus being tempted personally by the devil (Matthew 4:1-11) and (Luke 4:113). Throughout the rest of the scriptures we read about the subtle and devious temptations that Jesus faced. Yet, Jesus stood strong. He did not give in. In fact, Hebrews 4:16 talks of Jesus being tempted in every way that we have been tempted; and yet, he did not sin. That is why He knows that satan can make temptation so attractive and appealing to people, that it is difficult for them to resist him. Wherefore, in **James 4:7**, Jesus admonishes us and says *"Submit yourselves therefore to God. Resist the devil, and he will flee from you."*

The Bible also tells us that we do not face any temptations that others haven't faced before, and that God will never allow us to be tempted beyond what we can bear. Rather, when we are tempted, He will provide a way out so we can stand strong (1 Cor. 10:13). So when temptations come (and they will), there are three important things to do—

1. Ask God to help you.

2. Follow God's guidance so that you can be removed from the temptation; and,

3. Obey what He speaks to you.

It is not easy, but it is the only proven way to remove them. Sexual temptation is particularly difficult. **Sex** is a special **gift from God**, given to us to be experienced within the context of a loving **marriage relationship between a**

Man and a **Woman**. It is a powerful activity that brings a couple together and unites them very intimately. They become "one flesh."

Satan tries to convince us that if we do not indulge in pre-marital sex, then we are somehow missing out on life. But the truth is that sex, under such circumstances, does not really satisfy nor lead to a better relationship, despite what you see on television, at the movies, or what people may tell you.

It can lead to serial relationships and long term consequences. People cannot stop being *tempted* to have pre-marital sex because it is a "Natural" reaction to the attraction of the opposite sex, e.g., boy friend, girl friend, or fiancée. But for the sake of Godliness, Christians need to resist the temptation and the best way to do this is to pray and avoid all situations where it can lead to other things. Avoid being alone too much with the one you perceive to be the love of your life or your love interest.

The enemy has a favorite and effective tool called **LUST**, and the entertainment and fashion industry is eager to be partakers in the devil's attacks on every child, man, woman, boy, and girl!

Jesus tells us that He sends us out as sheep among wolves and that we are to be as **wise as serpents** and **harmless as doves**. We have to know what devices and tricks the devil is using and how he uses them if we want to be prepared to meet his challenges.

For example, these are a few of the tricks of his trade used to capture us if we remain unaware and unwise in our lifestyle choices:

1. Revealing clothing sales for women.
2. Exotic and enticing dances.
3. Pornography/Men Strip clubs.
4. The Internet.
5. Cell phones used to photograph the unsuspecting—
   - Sexting and texting
   - Facebook (inappropriate relationships)/gossiping
6. If you got it flaunt it.
7. Secrets: What happens in Vegas, stays in Vegas/ What they don't know won't hurt.
8. Just the right amount of wrong is ok as long as you don't overdo it.
9. A lie is as good as the truth if you can get someone to believe it.
10. Go ahead, take a sip, a puff, a pill, just one won't hurt you.
11. Prostitution, adultery, fornication, homosexuality.

Satan used a fruit to take down God's first two human creation, but today, he has so much more to use as bait:

SEX, DRUGS, PORN, ALCOHOL, GREED, WOMEN'S BREAST, TIGHTLY FITTED GARMENTS, SKIMPY CLOTHES, HOMOSEXUALLY, FORNICATION, ADULTERY, LYING, HATRED, DEPRESSION, ANXIETY, GLUTTONY, AND MENTAL ILLNESS.

A person may enjoy the pleasures of sin for a season, but in the end it leads to separation from God for eternity. The Prodigal Son learned all too well his lesson before he lost his soul. Had he not come to his senses and gone back home to his father's house, he might have been lost for eternity!

Choose today whom you will serve (**the fork in the road** leads to the left and to the right) The left leads to death, destruction, and eternity in hell. The right leads to Life and eternity in heaven. The choice is yours whether to stay on the right road with God or go down the wrong road to hell. Throw out those garments which so easily besets you! Do as Joshua did when he said:

AS FOR ME AND MY HOUSE, WE WILL SERVE THE LORD!

Keys To Success

His DIVINE POWER has given us EVERYTHING WE NEED for a godly life through our knowledge of Him who called us by His own glory and goodness. Through these he has given us his very great and precious promises, so that through them you may participate in the DIVINE NATURE, having escaped the corruption in the world caused by evil desires.

For this very reason, MAKE EVERY EFFORT to add to your ...

FAITH—a great vision

VIRTUE—a good heart

KNOWLEDGE—a hunger for truth

SELF-CONTROL—a willingness to change

STEADFASTNESS—a determination to stand

GODLINESS—a dependency on prayer

BROTHERLY AFFECTION—a passion for people

LOVE—a desire to please God

For if you possess these qualities in INCREASING MEASURE, they will KEEP YOU from being INEFFECTIVE and UNPRODUCTIVE in your knowledge of our Lord Jesus Christ.

But if any of you do not have them, you are NEARSIGHTED and BLIND, and you have FORGOTTEN that you have been cleansed from your past sins.

Therefore, my brothers and sisters, MAKE EVERY EFFORT to confirm your calling and election. For if you do these things, YOU WILL NEVER STUMBLE, and you will receive a rich welcome into the eternal kingdom of our Lord and Savior Jesus Christ.

Conclusion

*O*ur knowledge of God's goodness and His righteous judgments against evil should put the fear of God in us and help us not to indulge in sin. But even more so than that, the pure love for Him should do that also. It is imperative to be very careful when it comes to those things at which we look.

So much of the world's entertainment is designed to stir up lust and it is easy to stir up because it is pleasurable to the sinful human heart. Like Job, make a covenant with your eyes not to look with lust upon a young woman or young man (Job 31:1).

We may not be able to stop birds from flying over our head, but we can certainly stop them from making a nest in our hair. The devil has an effective way of dragging sinners to hell. He knows that many will hold onto sin, even if it means the death of them. Our calling as Christians are to encourage sinners to come to their senses—to let go of sin and escape the power of death!

Say the following quote to yourself:

There was a day when I died, utterly died--- (died to ****Place your name here's***** *opinions, preferences, tastes and will. Died to the world, its approval or censure. Died to the approval or blame even of my brethren and friends—and since then I have only to show myself approved of God."*

44

If we can overcome our fleshly desires, the world will have no attraction for us, and the devil will have no foothold on us. It is vital to identify this "Judas" in our hearts. Our old nature is nothing more than a cowardly traitor who will cry Master, Master,"and then betray the Son of God with a kiss. We must hang Judas by the neck until he has burst asunder in the midst, and all his bowels gushed out"(Acts 1:18). If we do not deal with this enemy, he will quietly steal from us until he betrays us and the cause for which we stand.

To defeat this enemy, we must consider ourselves to be dead to sin, and alive to God. We do this by not allowing sin to reign in our bodies. Rather than obeying it's lusts, we must yield ourselves fully to God and offer our bodies to Him as instruments of righteousness (Romans 6:11-13)

Satan will indeed keep inspiring the perverted fashions of this world. And unless we, as Christians, start or continue speaking up, out, and about it, the problems will only get worse. It's way overdue for Spirit filled laborers to answer their calls to service and be placed on the front lines of battle in this war of souls for Christ. God has called us all, as Christians, to be fishers of men. The time is now, and the harvest is plentiful, but the laborers are few.

My prayer is that this book has inspired many more to be fishermen who fish for souls! Christ says to be doers of the word and not just hearers, so I challenge you today to go out and practice what you preach! **"Preach the Word."**

2 Timothy 4:1-4New American Standard Bible (NASB)—[4] I solemnly charge *you* in the presence of God and of Christ Jesus, who is to judge the living and the dead, and by His appearing and His kingdom:[2] preach the word; be ready in season *and* out of season; reprove, rebuke, exhort, with [a]great patience and instruction. ³For the time will come when they will not endure sound doctrine; but *wanting* to have their ears tickled, they will accumulate for themselves teachers in accordance to their own desires, ⁴and will turn away their ears from the truth and will turn aside to myths.

We are the Salt and Light of the World

God calls us, as Christians, to be the salt and light of the world. He wants us to live in the world, but to be separate from it. Matthew 5:13-16 says "*You are the salt of the earth. But if the salt loses its saltiness, how can it be made salty again? It is no longer good for anything, except to be thrown out and trampled underfoot.. You are the light of the world. A town built on a hill cannot be hidden. Neither do people light a lamp and put it under a bowl. Instead they put it on its stand, and it gives light to everyone in the house. In the same way, let your light shine before others, that they may see your good deeds and glorify your Father in heaven.*"

Matthew 5:16 says "Let your light so shine before men, that they may see your good works, and glorify your Father which is in heaven."

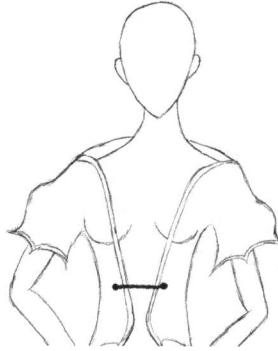

Let's talk about it!

Is It

Modest?

Is It

Godly?

	YES OR NO?	APPARELL	EXAMPLE
1	❏ YES ❏ NO	Exposed cleavage	
2	❏ YES ❏ NO	2 piece bikini	
3	❏ YES ❏ NO	Skimpy bathing suits	
4	❏ YES ❏ NO	Modest swimsuit for the pool or beach	
5	❏ YES ❏ NO	Tight fitting pants or skirt	
6	❏ YES ❏ NO	Tank tops	

	YES OR NO?	APPARELL	EXAMPLE
7	❑ YES ❑ NO	See thru tops	
8	❑ YES ❑ NO	Plunging neckline	
9	❑ YES ❑ NO	Knee length skirts	
10	❑ YES ❑ NO	Mini skirts	
11	❑ YES ❑ NO	Short shorts	
12	❑ YES ❑ NO	Writing across the seat of pants/on the bottom area	**SEXY**

	YES OR NO?	APPARELL	EXAMPLE
13	❑ YES ❑ NO	Cleavage Plunging neckline	
14	❑ YES ❑ NO	Cleavage	
15	❑ YES ❑ NO	Blouse	
16	❑ YES ❑ NO	Midriff	
17	❑ YES ❑ NO	Blouse	

What is acceptable swim wear for Christian women and young ladies???

Per the Bible, all bikinis are a no-no! Nothing Godly about it, ever—**Immodesty at its finest!!!) Don't be deceived or willfully disobedient!**

Bonus: A few "ladylike" tips!

When a woman or young lady bends over, it should always be with the knees bent, and not with the buttocks in the air (trust me, it happens!). It happens frequently; otherwise, I would not have included it in this section.

Young ladies, when bending over to pick up something, never bend over in front of a young man or man—not from the front or the back for this is not decent. This is your opportunity to allow him to be a gentleman. First, wait to see if he is going to respond by reaching down to retrieve the object. If not, politely ask him if he would retrieve the object for you. Always remember to thank him politely for his assistance, even if he doesn't help you.

And always, hold the front of your shirt close to your chest when bending down. Sit with your legs together whether wearing pants/skirt or dress—**always**!

Try layering your shirts for a nice look and to cover your cleavage, especially if it has a low neckline. More attention will be focused on the outer shirt!

SALVATION— The Best Gift You Can Ever Receive If You Desire It!

If you Died Tonight, Where Would You Go?

Question Your Future

You don't know? You're not sure? Would you like to go to Heaven? Would you like to live forever in perfect peace with your Creator? How can you be sure you have a place reserved for you in Heaven?

ADMIT

Admit that you are a sinner. Sin is choosing to disobey God and not follow His will (what He wants us to do). Romans 3:23—for all have sinned and fall short of the glory of God

We are separated from God because of our sin. We deserve eternal (forever) death or separation from God.

Romans 6:23—For the wages of sin is death, but the free gift of God is eternal life in Christ Jesus our Lord.

UNDERSTAND

Understand who Jesus is. Jesus Christ is the Son of God and He is God. He is your only way to God the Father.

John 14:6—Jesus said to him, "I am the way, and the truth, and the life; no one comes to the Father but through Me."

Understand what Jesus did for you. By Jesus' death on the

cross, He paid for our sins. Jesus our Savior means He saves us from eternal (forever) punishment for our sins.

Romans 5:8—But God demonstrates His own love toward us, in that while we were yet sinners, Christ died for us. John 3:16—For God so loved the world, that He gave His only begotten Son, that whoever believes in Him shall not perish, but have eternal life.

BELIEVE

Believe in Jesus—Believe who Jesus is. Believe that he died for you and that He is your Savior. Believe that He is the only way to Heaven. Believe that He is your Lord and that you owe Him your life.

REPENT

Repent of your sins. Allow the Holy Spirit to show all your sins to you. Confess and repent (agree to turn away from them).

Acts 3:19—Repent ye therefore, and be converted, that your sins may be blotted out, when the times of refreshing shall come from the presence of the Lord.

Romans 10:9—that if you confess with your mouth Jesus as Lord, and believe in your heart that God raised Him from the dead, you will be saved.

COMMIT

Commit to God's plan of salvation from sin and reconciliation with Him by praying a prayer like this:

"Dear God, I know I'm a sinner. Please forgive me. I believe that Jesus died for my sins. I want Jesus to come into my life and be my Savior. I don't want to live for myself

anymore. I want to follow Him and obey Him. I want Him to be the Lord of my life."

If you understood and truthfully lifted this up in prayer to God, then all of Heaven is celebrating now, you are a new Christian and you have a place reserved for you in Heaven!

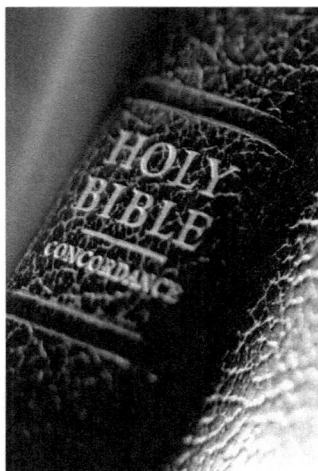

Daily Prayer

Matthew 6:9-13 (KJV)

[9] After this manner therefore pray ye: Our Father which art in heaven, Hallowed be thy name.

[10] Thy kingdom come, Thy will be done in earth, as it is in heaven.

[11] Give us this day our daily bread.

[12] And forgive us our debts, as we forgive our debtors.

[13] And lead us not into temptation, but deliver us from evil: For thine is the kingdom, and the power, and the glory, for ever. Amen.

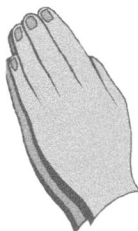

Promises to us who die in this life as children of God

John 3:16 (NIV)

¹⁶ For God so loved the world that he gave his one and only Son, that whoever believes in him shall not perish but have eternal life.

John 14:2-3 (NIV)

2 My Father's house has many rooms; if that were not so, would I have told you that I am going there to prepare a place for you? **3 And if I go and prepare a place for you, I will come back and take you to be with me that you also may be where I am.**

Living for the day when we hear our Father say:

"Well done you Good and Faithful Servants, enter into your reward!"

These are the words we all should long to hear.

NOT

"Depart from me, I never knew you!"

<u>**TAKE INVENTORY:**</u>

How are you Living?

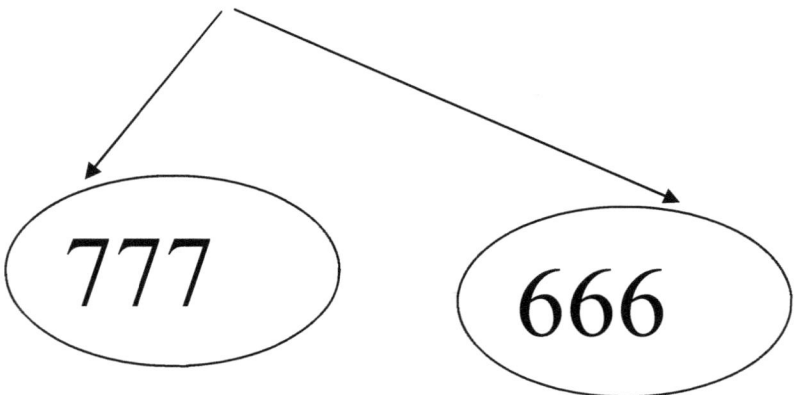

777   666

Quick Scriptural References

Acknowledgements

Thank You!
Thank You!
Thank You!

TO:

Pappi—God, my awesome Father!!!!

Jesus—For loving us all so much that you lived and died for our sins!

The Holy Spirit—For living inside of me!

My Husband and Kiddos—You all are super young men and young women and we're blessed to be able to raise you. I'm looking forward to seeing more great things from you!...And You, Mr. Russell ☺, for your endless amount of encouragement and patience! You truly do have the patience of a saint! We all make a great team!

Mom—For your kindness and tender heart

Aunt Nita—For the strength as a woman that you instilled within me!

Momma Fannie—For your unwavering faith in God!

Aunt Mammie—RIP! For your selflessness!

Grandma Earsie—For the work ethic you passed on to me!

Uncle Justice—For your wisdom!

Mrs. Smith (Woodridge Elementary DeSoto, TX)—The epitome of what a Godly/Modest Woman looks and behaves like!

Lori— For your knowledge!

Aleria—Gifted artist!

Brother in Law Robert—Gifted Artist!

Pastor Chris and Tiffany Faggins (Pastor and 1st Lady) —Favored with Hope, Owners

Mrs. Ida Malone Jackson, ROOTS—Typesetting/Layout/ Design

Grandpa Rooters—aka "Rev Rootie." I felt your presence the entire time I was writing this book!—(RIP)

And lastly (satan)—because I love finding new and interesting ways to stomp on your face and snatch souls from your hell.

Amen

About the Author

Evangelist Angelia Russell was raised in Seattle, Washington and now resides in a quiet suburb of Dallas, Texas with her husband Keith Russell of Oklahoma City and their Children. Together they have 7: Ashton, Tarren, Talen, Hunter, Mia, Spencer, Anna and one grandchild Braelen (born in 2013).

Mrs. Russell was born into a family of successful entrepreneurs and along with her husband Keith, is the owner of a dental staffing agency in DeSoto, Texas. She also works and volunteers at "*Favored With Hope,* a non-profit agency whose primary goal is to bring about community change from within and provide quality on-going services to at-risk youths and seniors.

Mrs. Russell is also a nature lover and an avid reader.

To contact the author, write to:

A. Russell

512 N. Hampton Rd #252

DeSoto, TX 75115

COMING
SOON

Children's version of

FIG Leaves